# Weeping from the Fear of Allaah

*by*
Shaykh Husayn al-'Awaayishah

*Translated by*
Bint Feroz Din & Bint 'Abd al-Ghafoor

ISBN 1 898649 33 2

British Library Cataloguing in Publication Data.
A catalogue record for this book is available from the British Library.

First Edition, 1419 AH/1998 CE

Cover design:     Abu Yahya

Typeset by:       Al-Hidaayah Publishing and Distribution Ltd

Published by:     Al-Hidaayah Publishing and Distribution Ltd
                  P.O. Box 3332
                  Birmingham
                  United Kingdom
                  B10 0UH

                  Tel: 0121 753 1889
                  Fax: 0121 753 2422
                  E-Mail: mail@al-hidaayah.co.uk
                  Internet: www.al-hidaayah.co.uk

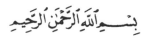

# Publisher's Note

All praise is for Allaah, Lord of the worlds. Peace and prayers be upon Muhammad, his family, his Companions and all those who follow in their footsteps until the Last Day.

In your hands is an English translation of the Arabic booklet, *al-Bukaa'u min Khashyatillaah* by Shaykh Husayn al-'Awaayishah who is one of the students of Shaykh Muhammad Naasiruddeen al-Albaanee.*

In his usual style, the author has adorned his book with verses of the Qur'aan, sayings of the Prophet (ﷺ), examples of the Companions and reports from the pious predecessors. We pray that the heart rendering narrations that the author has so carefully chosen will act as a means of softening our hearts, purifying our souls and permanently changing our outlook on our short lives in this world.

We would like to thank all the bothers and sisters who helped in this project - may Allaah reward them for their hard work!

*Al-Hidaayah Publishing and Distribution*

---

* Thus whenever the author refers to "our Shaykh" he is referring to Shaykh al-Albaanee.

# Contents

# Introduction

All praise is for Allaah. We praise Him and seek His help and forgiveness. We seek refuge in Allaah from the evil of our own selves and from our evil actions. Whomsoever Allaah guides, there is none to misguide him, and whomsoever Allaah leads astray none can guide him aright. I testify that none has the right to be worshipped except Allaah, alone with no partner, and I testify that Muhammad (ﷺ) is His slave and messenger.

يَـٰٓأَيُّهَا ٱلَّذِينَ ءَامَنُواْ ٱتَّقُواْ ٱللَّهَ حَقَّ تُقَاتِهِۦ وَلَا تَمُوتُنَّ إِلَّا وَأَنتُم مُّسۡلِمُونَ ﴿١٠٢﴾

**O you who believe! Fear Allaah as He should be feared and die not except as Muslims (in a state of Islaam with complete submission to Allaah).**[1]

يَـٰٓأَيُّهَا ٱلنَّاسُ ٱتَّقُواْ رَبَّكُمُ ٱلَّذِى خَلَقَكُم مِّن نَّفۡسٍ وَٰحِدَةٍ وَخَلَقَ مِنۡهَا زَوۡجَهَا وَبَثَّ مِنۡهُمَا رِجَالًا كَثِيرًا وَنِسَآءً وَٱتَّقُواْ ٱللَّهَ ٱلَّذِى تَسَآءَلُونَ بِهِۦ وَٱلۡأَرۡحَامَ إِنَّ ٱللَّهَ كَانَ عَلَيۡكُمۡ رَقِيبًا ﴿١﴾

**O mankind! Be dutiful to your Lord, Who created you from a single person (Aadam), and from him (Aadam) He created his wife (Eve), and from them both He created many men and women, and fear Allaah through whom you demand your mutual (rights), and (do not cut the relations of) the wombs (kinship). Surely, Allaah is Ever an All-Watcher over you.**[2]

---

[1] Soorah Aali-'Imraan (3):102.

[2] Soorah an-Nisaa' (4):1.

يَٰٓأَيُّهَا ٱلَّذِينَ ءَامَنُوا۟ ٱتَّقُوا۟ ٱللَّهَ وَقُولُوا۟ قَوْلًا سَدِيدًا ۝ يُصْلِحْ لَكُمْ أَعْمَٰلَكُمْ وَيَغْفِرْ لَكُمْ ذُنُوبَكُمْ وَمَن يُطِعِ ٱللَّهَ وَرَسُولَهُۥ فَقَدْ فَازَ فَوْزًا عَظِيمًا ۝

**O you who believe! Keep your duty to Allaah and fear Him, and speak the truth. He will direct you towards righteous good deeds and will forgive you your sins. And whosoever obeys Allaah and His Messenger, he has indeed achieved a great achievement.**[3]

Indeed the best speech is the book of Allaah, and the best guidance is that of Muhammad (ﷺ). The worst affairs are the newly invented matters, for every newly invented matter is an innovation, every innovation is misguidance, and every misguidance is in the Fire.

People are distressed and feel repressed by sins. Their hardened hearts have prevented their eyes from producing tears and weeping and they have been forbidden the pleasure and sweetness of *eemaan*, except those whom Allaah has been merciful to, and how few they are!

I therefore saw an urgent need to address this topic, and thereby express the virtue and excellence of weeping out of fear of Allaah, the Most High, and to clarify the path towards achieving this. Furthermore, to overcome the obstacles one may face, to the best of one's ability. So I have mentioned some of the texts and narrations about the weeping of the Prophet Muhammad (ﷺ) and his Companions, (may Allaah be pleased with them all).

---

[3]  Soorah al-Ahzaab (33):70-71.

I cannot fail to thank my honourable Shaykh, Muḥammad Naaṣirud-Deen al-Albaanee (may Allaah preserve him), for benefiting me on this topic with the reports and extracts from his book *Ṣaheeh at-Targheeb wat Tarheeb* which is in manuscript form and which have yet to be printed.

I ask Allaah, the Most High, to accept my work and to not let anyone have a share of it (i.e., for it to be sincerely for Allaah alone). Indeed Allaah has power over all things.

# Weeping out of Fear of Allaah

Allaah, the Most High, says:

$$اللَّهُ نَزَّلَ أَحْسَنَ الْحَدِيثِ كِتَابًا مُّتَشَبِهًا مَّثَانِى تَقْشَعِرُّ مِنْهُ جُلُودُ الَّذِينَ يَخْشَوْنَ رَبَّهُمْ ثُمَّ تَلِينُ جُلُودُهُمْ وَقُلُوبُهُمْ إِلَىٰ ذِكْرِ اللَّهِ$$

**Allaah has sent down the best statement, a Book (this Qur'aan) its parts resembling each other in goodness and truth oft repeated. The skins of those who fear their Lord shiver from it. Then their skins and hearts soften to the remembrance of Allaah.**[4]

Allaah, the Most High, says:

$$إِنَّ الَّذِينَ أُوتُوا الْعِلْمَ مِن قَبْلِهِ إِذَا يُتْلَىٰ عَلَيْهِمْ يَخِرُّونَ لِلْأَذْقَانِ سُجَّدًا ۩ وَيَقُولُونَ سُبْحَانَ رَبِّنَا إِن كَانَ وَعْدُ رَبِّنَا لَمَفْعُولًا ۩ وَيَخِرُّونَ لِلْأَذْقَانِ يَبْكُونَ وَيَزِيدُهُمْ خُشُوعًا ۩$$

**Those who were given knowledge before it (i.e., the Jews and Christians) when it is recited to them, fall down on their faces in humble prostration. And they say glory be to our Lord! Truly the promise of our Lord must be fulfilled. And they fall down on their faces weeping and it adds to their humility.**[5]

---

[4] Soorah az-Zumar (39):23.

[5] Soorah al-Israa' (17):107-109.

Allaah, the Most High, says:

$$\text{أُوْلَٰٓئِكَ ٱلَّذِينَ}$$

$$\text{أَنْعَمَ ٱللَّهُ عَلَيْهِم مِّنَ ٱلنَّبِيِّـۧنَ مِن ذُرِّيَّةِ ءَادَمَ وَمِمَّنْ حَمَلْنَا مَعَ نُوحٍ}$$

$$\text{وَمِن ذُرِّيَّةِ إِبْرَٰهِيمَ وَإِسْرَٰٓءِيلَ وَمِمَّنْ هَدَيْنَا وَٱجْتَبَيْنَآ إِذَا تُتْلَىٰ عَلَيْهِمْ}$$

$$\text{ءَايَٰتُ ٱلرَّحْمَٰنِ خَرُّوا۟ سُجَّدًا وَبُكِيًّا ۩ ﴿٥٨﴾}$$

**They were those unto whom Allaah bestowed His Grace, from among the prophets, of the offspring of Aadam, and of those whom We carried (in the ship) with Noo<u>h</u> and of the offspring of Ibraaheem and Israa'eel and from among those whom we guided and chose. When the verses of the most Gracious were recited unto them, they fell down prostrating and weeping.**[6]

It has been related on the authority of Aboo Hurayrah (*radiyallaahu 'anhu*) who said: *I heard the Messenger of Allaah (ﷺ) say: "Seven will be granted the shade of Allaah on a day when there will be no shade*[7] *but His. A just ruler,*[8] *a youth who has been brought up wor-*

---

[6] Soorah Maryam (19):58.

[7] Our Shaykh al-Albaanee says in *at-Targheeb wat Tarheeb* (1/1440): The attribution of the shade to Allaah is an attribution of ownership. Every shade is His shade, His property, His creation and authority [i.e., Allaah owns this shade. The point being stressed here is that it is not an attribution of a characteristic to Allaah. Rather, this type of attribution is similar to "slave of Allaah" or "house of Allaah" etc. So the shade is not an attribute of Allaah but it has been annexed to Him for purposes of distinction and nobility which therefore sets it apart from all other shades]. What is meant here is the shade of the Throne as it has been clearly mentioned in another hade*eth*. The day that is referred to is the Day of Resurrection, when the people stand in front of the Lord of the Worlds, and the sun draws close to them, and they feel the intense heat and begin to perspire. There will not be any shade (on that Day) except the shade of the Throne.

*shipping Allaah, a man whose heart is attached to the mosque,[9] two people who love each other for the sake of Allaah and meet and part upon that,[10] a man who is allured by a woman of high standing and beauty and he says 'I fear Allaah',[11] one who gives charity in secret so that his left hand does not know what his right hand has given, and a man whose eyes fill up with tears when he remembers Allaah in private."[12]*

Also on the authority of Aboo Hurayrah (*radiyallaahu 'anhu*) who heard the Messenger of Allaah (ﷺ) say: *"The fire will not touch a man who weeps out of the fear of Allaah until the milk returns to the*

---

[8] Our Shaykh al-Albaanee says in *at-Targheeb wat Tarheeb* (1/1440): That is anyone from among the people in authority, who is concerned with the welfare and good of the Muslims Indeed, the *hadeeth* begins with mentioning the just ruler (before anybody else) because of his abundant benefit to more people (than any of the other people mentioned). It is necessary for the one who rules to adhere to the Qur'aan and *Sunnah* because without that he cannot be just, so be aware of this.

[9] Our Shaykh al-Albaanee says in *at-Targheeb wat Tarheeb* (1/1440): Meaning he has a strong love for the Mosques and he perseveres in attending the congregational prayers in them.

[10] Our Shaykh al-Albaanee says in *at-Targheeb wat Tarheeb* (1/1440): The meaning of 'meeting for the sake of Allaah and parting for the sake of Allaah' is that the reason for their meeting is due to their love of Allaah and they both remain upon that (love) until they part from their meeting, each of them believing that their love is for the sake of Allaah. And this is their condition upon meeting and upon parting.

[11] al-Albaanee says in *at-Targheeb wat Tarheeb* (1/1440): This may be the saying of the tongue or with the heart, in order to restrain his soul and hold back from this woman of high status and beauty. The woman of high status and beauty was mentioned especially because she is more desired, and more difficult to get. It appears that he said it with his heart and his tongue.

[12] Reported by al-Bukhaaree, Muslim and others. Refer to *Saheeh at-Targheeb* (1/201) for further benefits related to this *hadeeth*.

*breasts. Also the dust produced in Jihaad and the smoke of hell will never co-exist."*[13]

On the authority of Ibn 'Abbaas (*radiyallaahu 'anhumaa*) who heard the Messenger of Allaah (ﷺ) say: *"There are two eyes which will not be touched by the Fire: an eye which weeps out of the fear of Allaah and an eye which stays vigil throughout the night guarding for the sake of Allaah."*[14]

On the authority of Aboo Hurayrah (*radiyallaahu 'anhu*) that the Messenger of Allaah (ﷺ) said: *"Two eyes have been forbidden from being overcome by the Fire. An eye which has wept out of the fear of Allaah and an eye which stays vigil throughout the night guarding Islaam and one's family from Kufr."* [15]

On the authority of Aboo Umaamah (*radiyallaahu 'anhu*) that the Prophet (ﷺ) said: *"There is nothing more beloved to Allaah (the Most High) than two drops and two marks. A teardrop shed out of fear of Allaah (the Most High) and a drop of blood spilt for the sake of Allaah (the Most High). As for the two marks, one which is sustained for the sake of Allaah and one which is received in the course of carrying out an obligation commanded by Allaah (the Most High)."*[16]

---

[13] Reported by at-Tirmidhee, who said it is a *hasan saheeh* hadeeth. Also reported by an-Nasaa'ee and al-Haakim who said it has a *saheeh* (authentic) chain of narration. Also refer to: *at-Targheeb wal Tarheeb by al-Mundhiree.* It was declared authentic by our Shaykh in *al-Mishkaat* (3828) and in *at-Targheeb wal Tarheeb.*

[14] Reported by at-Tirmidhee, and our Shaykh declared it *saheeh* in *al-Mishkaat* and in *Saheeh at-Targheeb.*

[15] Reported by al-Haakim in *al-Mustadrak* and by others. Declared *saheeh* by our Shaykh in *Saheeh at-Targheeb.*

[16] Reported by at-Tirmidhee who said it is *hasan*, our Shaykh said it has a *hasan* chain of narration, in *al-Mishkaat* and in *Saheeh at-Targheeb.*

On the authority of 'Uthmaan (*radiyallaahu 'anhu*) who said that the Messenger of Allaah (ﷺ) said: *"Toobah[17] is for anyone who controls his tongue, whose house is sufficient for him (i.e., he is content with it) and who weeps over his errors."*[18]

On the authority of 'Uqbah ibn 'Aamir (*radiyallaahu 'anhu*) who asked: *'I said, "O Messenger of Allaah! What is salvation?" He replied: "To have control over your tongue, to be content with your house and to weep over your errors."'*[19]

---

[17] It is a tree in Paradise whose course runs the distance of a hundred years. The clothing of the people of Paradise is extracted from its from within it. From his (ﷺ)' statement: *"Toobah is a tree in Paradise, its course runs the distance of a hundred years, and the clothing of the people of paradise is extracted from within it."* Reported by Ahmad and others, it is *hasan li ghayrihee*, reported by our Shaykh in *as-Saheehah*.

[18] Reported by at-Tabraanee in *al-Awsat as-Sagheer* and he declared its chain of narration to be *hasan* as al-Mundhiree related it in *at-Targheeb wat Tarheeb*. And our *Shaykh* declared it *hasan in Saheeh at-Targheeb*.

[19] Reported by Ibn al-Mubaarak in *az-Zuhd*, by Ahmad, at-Tirmidhee and others. It is a *saheeh hadeeth* and reported by our Shaykh in *as-Saheehah*.

# Beware of the Hardness of the Heart

Beware of the hardness of the heart, for it can lead you to the Fire. So protect your heart from becoming hard and all that which may cause it to harden, and beware of turning away from the admonition of Allaah, the Most High.

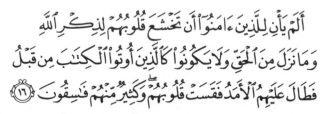

**Has not the time come for the hearts of those who believe to be affected by Allaah's Reminder (this Qur'aan) and that which has been revealed of the truth, lest they become as those who received the Scripture before, and the term was prolonged for them and so their hearts were hardened? And many of them were rebellious, disobedient (*faasiqoon*).**[20]

It has been mentioned in an explanation of this verse, which has been reported by Aboo Haazim, that 'Aamir ibn 'Abdullaah ibn az-Zubayr related to him (i.e., Aboo Haazim) that his father informed him that only four years had passed between the time of their acceptance of Islaam, and the revelation of this verse, through which Allaah was reproaching them:

وَلَا يَكُونُوا۟ كَالَّذِينَ أُوتُوا۟ ٱلْكِتَٰبَ مِن قَبْلُ فَطَالَ عَلَيْهِمُ ٱلْأَمَدُ فَقَسَتْ قُلُوبُهُمْ وَكَثِيرٌ مِّنْهُمْ فَٰسِقُونَ ﴿١٦﴾

---

[20] Soorah al-Hadeed (57):16.

**…lest they become as those who received the Scrip-
ture before, and the term was prolonged for them
and so their hearts were hardened? And many of
them were rebellious, disobedient (*faasiqoon*).**[21]

Ibn 'Abbaas also said in an explanation of this verse: 'They became
inclined to this world and turned away from the admonition of
Allaah.'[22]

---

[21] *Saheeh* in *Sunan ibn Maajah*

[22] Al-Baghawee has mentioned it in his *tafseer*.

# Weeping[23] is a Mercy which Allaah puts in the Hearts of His Servants

On the authority of Usaamah ibn Zayd (*ra<u>d</u>iyallaahu 'anhumaa*) who said: '*We were with the Prophet (ﷺ) when one of his daughters sent a messenger calling for him, informing him that her small child, or her son, was dying. So the Prophet (ﷺ) told the messenger: "Return to her and inform her, that whatever Allaah takes and gives belongs to Him and that everything has an appointed term, so let her be patient and anticipate Allaah's reward in the Hereafter." Later the messenger returned to the Prophet (ﷺ), and said: 'Verily she has sworn by Allaah that you come to her.' So the Prophet (ﷺ) got up and so too did Sa'ad ibn 'Ubaadah and Mu'aadh ibn Jabal, and I too went with them. The small boy was lifted up to the Prophet (ﷺ), and let out a groaning noise,[24] as if he was breathing his last*

---

23  Ibn al-Qayyim said: "The types of weeping are:

1) The weeping of mercy and compassion. 2) The weeping of fear and reverence. 3) The weeping of love and longing. 4) The weeping of joy and happiness. 5) The weeping of worry and anguish brought about by pain, and the inability to bear it. 6) The weeping of sadness. 7) The weeping of fatigue and weakness. 8) The weeping of hypocrisy, that is when the eyes fill up with tears, while the heart is hard. 9) The weeping of the false and the hired, such as the woman who wails to be paid. [**Translators note:** It was an old Arab custom in pre-Islamic Arabia, to hire people to attend someone's funeral, in order to cry and wail, and cause much commotion and noise, to make it appear to other people that the deceased was very much liked and missed. The Prophet (ﷺ) later condemned this]. 10) the weeping of agreement, that is when a person sees other people crying over something that has happened to them, so he too starts to cry, not knowing why they are crying." (*Zaad al-Ma'aad* - with slight abridgement)

24  The groaning noise (*al-qa'qa'*): the movement of something, from which a noise is heard. The meaning intended here is agitation and movement. He (i.e., the narrator) meant: Each time the child entered upon a particular state it did not take long before he entered upon another which brings him closer to death. Refer to *an-Nihaayah*.

*breath.*[25] *Thereby the Prophet's (ﷺ) eyes over-flowed with tears. Upon this Sa'ad asked: 'What is this, O Messenger of Allaah?' He (ﷺ) replied: "This is a mercy, which Allaah puts in the hearts of His servants. And verily Allaah shows mercy to those of His servants who are merciful."*[26]

---

[25] The noise of breathing when one breathes into a very old vessel.

[26] Reported by al-Bukhaaree and Muslim.

# The Weeping of the Prophet Muhammad (ﷺ)[27]

On the authority of 'Abdullaah ibn Mas'ood (*radiyallaahu 'anhumaa*), who said: '*The Messenger of Allaah (ﷺ) told me: "Re-cite to me!" So I recited Soorah an-Nisaa', until I reached:*

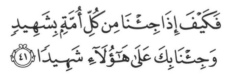

**How will it be then, when We bring from each na-tion a witness, and We bring you (O Prophet Muhammad) as a witness against these people?[28]**

*Then I looked towards him, and behold! I saw that his eyes were overflowing with tears.'[29]*

An explanation of this noble verse has been mentioned in a *hadeeth* related by Aboo Sa'eed (*radiyallaahu 'anhu*) who said that the Messenger of Allaah (ﷺ) said: *"A prophet will come and with him will be two men, and (another) prophet will come and with him will be three men, and more and less than that. It will be said to him: 'Did you convey (the message) to your nation?' he will reply: "Yes" then his nation will be called, and it will be said to them: 'Was the*

---

[27]  Ibn al-Qayyim said in *Zaad al-Ma'aad*: 'As for the weeping of the Prophet (ﷺ), it was in the same degree as his laughter. He wouldn't sob loudly and raise his voice, just like his laughter wasn't loud. However his eyes would fill up with tears, until they flowed out, and you would hear the sound like that of a whistling kettle coming from his chest. He would weep out of mercy for the dead, out of fear and compassion for his *Ummah*, out of deep fear of Allaah, upon listening to the Qur'aan. And it was a weeping of longing, love and exaltation, accompanied by fear and *khashyah*".

[28]  Soorah an-Nisaa' (4):41.

[29]  Reported by al-Bukhaaree, Muslim and others.

*message conveyed to you?' and they will reply: "No." So it will be
said (to that prophet) 'Who will testify for you?' He will reply:
'Muhammad (ﷺ) and his nation.' So the nation of Muhammad (ﷺ)
will be called and it will be said to them: 'Were you informed of
this?' and they will reply: 'Yes.' So it will be asked: 'How did you
come to know about that?' and they will reply: "Our Prophet (ﷺ)
informed us that the messengers (before him) had conveyed the
message, and we believed him." He (Aboo Sa'eed) said: 'So that is
what Allaah (the Most High) means when He says in the Qur'aan:*

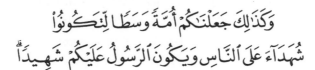

...**and thus We have made you (Muslims-real believers) a just nation that you be witnesses over
mankind, and the Messenger (Prophet Muhammad)
be a witness over you...**[30], [31]

On the authority of 'Alee (*radiyallaahu 'anhu*), who said: *'We did
not have a horseman with us on the day of Badr except al-Miqdaad.
Everyone amongst us was sleeping except for the Messenger of
Allaah (ﷺ) who was under a tree, praying and weeping until the
morning.'*[32]

On the authority of 'Abdullaah ibn 'Amr (*radiyallaahu 'anhu*) who
said: *'One day, during the lifetime of the Messenger of Allaah (ﷺ)
the sun eclipsed, so he stood and prayed, until it seemed as though*

---

[30] Soorah al-Baqarah (2):143.

[31] Reported by Ibn Maajah, Ahmad and al-Bukhaaree reported something similar
to it, and it is in *as-Saheehah*.

[32] Reported by Ibn Khuzaymah in his *Saheeh*. And our *Shaykh* declared it *saheeh*
in *Saheeh at-Targheeb wat Tarheeb*.

*he wouldn't go into rukoo' (the bowing position), then he went into rukoo' (for such a long time) that it seemed as if he wouldn't raise his head, then he raised his head. He remained (in that position) and it seemed as if he wouldn't go into sujood (the prostrating position), then he made sajdah (prostration), and (he remained in that position) until it seemed as if he wouldn't raise his head, then he raised his head, and it seemed as if he wouldn't go into sujood again, then he made sajdah, until it seemed as if he wouldn't raise his head again. Then he began to breathe heavily and weep, saying: "Lord, didn't You promise me that You wouldn't punish them while I am amongst them? Lord didn't You promise me that You wouldn't punish them while they seek forgiveness from you, and we seek forgiveness from you?" When he had finished praying two rak'ah, the sun eclipse had cleared, and he (﷽) got up and praised and glorified Allaah and then he said: "The sun and the moon are two signs from among the signs of Allaah, they do not eclipse because of the death or life of anyone. So if you see them eclipse, then hasten to the remembrance of Allaah."*[33]

On the authority of al-Baraa ibn 'Aazib (*radiyallaahu 'anhu*) who said: *'While we were with the Messenger of Allaah (﷽), he suddenly looked towards a group (of people) and said: "For what reason have they gathered here?" It was said 'In order to dig a grave.'*

---

[33] Mentioned in *ash-Shamaa'il al-Muhammadeeyah*. Reported by an-Nasaa'ee in *Salaat il-Kusoof*. Our Shaykh said in *Mukhtasar ash-Shamaa'il:* 'Aboo Daawood reported it, see *Saheeh Aboo Daawood,* and in *Irwaa al-Ghaleel,* some of them said it has a *saheeh* chain of narration. And there are two *rukoo'* in every *raka'h*, this is what is preserved (*mahfoodh*) in the *ahaadeeth* of the eclipse in the two *Saheeh*'s and by others, on the authority of Ibn 'Amr and others, just as it is clarified in the two mentioned sources. And I have separated it, into a booklet called '*Sifah Salaat il-Kusoof*'(A Description of the Prayer of the Eclipse). Hence what is in the narration of the book; that *rukoo'* is only mentioned once, this is a weak narration that opposes stronger narrations.'

*So the Messenger of Allaah (ﷺ) became alarmed and startled and he quickly went ahead of his Companions until he reached the grave, then he knelt upon it, and I turned my face towards him (ﷺ), in order to see what he was doing. He (ﷺ) cried until the earth became wet with his tears, then he turned to us and said: "O my brothers! Prepare for a day like this."*[34]

On the authority of 'Abdullaah ibn ash-Shikh-kheer (*radiyallaahu 'anhu*) who said: '*I saw the Messenger of Allaah (ﷺ) praying with us, and I heard the sound of his weeping coming out of his chest, which was like the sound of a boiling pot.*'[35]

---

[34] Reported by al-Bukhaaree in *at-Taareekh*, Ibn Maajah, Ahmad and others. It is a *hasan hadeeth* which our Shaykh related in *as-Saheehah*.

[35] Reported by Aboo Daawood, an-Nasaa'ee and at-Tirmidhee in *ash-Shamaa'il* and al-Haafidh said in *al-Fath*: it has a strong chain of narration. Declared authentic by Ibn Khuzaymah, Ibn Hibbaan and al-Haakim. And our Shaykh declared it authentic in *at-Targheeb wat Tarheeb*.

# The Weeping of the Companions (*radiyallaahu 'anhum*)

On the authority of al-'Irbaad ibn Saariyah (*radiyallaahu 'anhu*) who said: '*The Messenger of Allaah (ﷺ) gave us a profound admonition, which caused our hearts to tremble, and our eyes to shed tears. So we said: "O Messenger of Allaah (ﷺ) it is as if you have given us a farewell sermon, so counsel us." He (ﷺ) replied: "I advise you to have taqwa of Allaah, and to hear and obey, even if an Abyssinian slave is put in authority over you. And whoever of you lives (long enough), he will see much differing. Then it is incumbent upon you to stick to my Sunnah, and the Sunnah of the rightly guided Caliphs. And bite on to it with your molar teeth.*[36] *Beware of newly invented matters, for verily, every innovation is a misguidance."*'[37]

On the authority of Anas (*radiyallaahu 'anhu*) who said: '*The Messenger of Allaah (ﷺ) gave us a sermon, the like of which we had never heard before. He (ﷺ) said: "If you knew what I know you would laugh little and weep much!" Thereupon the Companions of the Prophet (ﷺ) covered their faces, weeping and sniffing*[38] .'[39]

---

[36] Meaning: Cling firmly to the *sunnah* and strive towards it, just like the one who bites would cling on to something with his molar teeth, fearing that it may slip away and escape.

[37] Reported by Aboo Daawood, at-Tirmidhee, Ibn Maajah and others. Refer to *Saheeh Sunan Ibn Maajah*, *Saheeh Sunan Aboo Daawood* and *Saheeh Sunan at-Tirmidhee*, also see *Saheeh at-Targheeb wat Tarheeb* and the *takhreej* of *Kitaab as-Sunnah*.

[38] Meaning: They made the sound of weeping without sobbing. The Arabic word used is *khaneen*, meaning: a sound which issues from the nose, like the *khaneen* which issues from the mouth (*an-Nihaayah*). Al-Haafidh says in *al-Fath:* It is reported as *Haneen* with a *h* by most of those who related *Saheeh al-Bukhaaree* and al-Kashmeehanee related it as *khaneen* with a *kh*; the first refers to the sound that emanates from weeping of the chest and the second, from the nose.

[39] Reported by al-Bukhaaree and Muslim.

# The Weeping of Aboo Bakr (*radiyallaahu 'anhu*)

Aboo Bakr's recitation in prayer could not be heard due to his excessive weeping, as we have been informed by 'Aa'ishah (*radiyallaahu 'anhaa*), who said: '*During his illness, the Messenger of Allaah (ﷺ) said: "Order Aboo Bakr to lead the prayer."* '*Aa'ishah said: "I told the Messenger of Allaah (ﷺ), that indeed , if Aboo Bakr stands in your place (to lead the people in prayer) the people will not be able to hear him due to his (excessive) weeping. So order 'Umar to lead the prayer." The Prophet (ﷺ) said again: "Order Aboo Bakr to lead the prayer." Then 'Aa'ishah told Hafsah: "Tell the Messenger of Allaah (ﷺ) that if Aboo Bakr stands in your place, the people will not be able to hear him due to his weeping, so order 'Umar to lead the people in prayer." So Hafsah did this and the Prophet (ﷺ) replied: "Desist! Verily you are like the companions of Yoosuf.*[40] *Order Aboo Bakr to lead the prayer." Then Hafsah said to 'Aa'ishah: "You have never done any good for me."*'[41]

---

[40] Al-Haafidh said in *al-Fath*: 'The similarity between 'Aa'ishah and the people of Yoosuf was that the wife of the 'Azeez had invited some of the women (of her town) apparently to honour them with a royal feast, but her real motive was that she wanted to exhibit the rare beauty of Yoosuf to them. And 'Aa'ishah's apparent motive for requesting the Prophet (ﷺ) to spare her father from the responsibility of leading the people in prayer, was that (due to his being a very sensitive man) the faithful would not be able to hear his recitation due to his weeping (whilst reciting) in the prayer. However, the more complete meaning here is (her real motive was, that she feared) that other people might see a bad omen in him (in case of the death of the Prophet (ﷺ)). It is reported by al-Bukhaaree, on the authority of 'Aa'ishah, who said: '*I persisted in my request to the Messenger of Allaah (ﷺ) with regards to this as much as I could. Because it never entered my heart that the people could ever love a man who took the Messenger of Allaah's (ﷺ) place. I used to think that the people would only see a bad omen in anyone who took his place, so I wanted the Messenger of Allaah to change his mind about (appointing) Aboo Bakr (in his position).*' Also reported in Muslim.

[41] Reported by al-Bukhaaree.

And in another narration: *'Indeed Aboo Bakr is a man of tender feelings, if he takes your place he will not be able to lead the people in prayer.'*[42]

---

[42] Reported by al-Bukhaaree.

# The Weeping of 'Umar (*radiyallaahu 'anhu*)

The weeping of 'Umar (*radiyallaahu 'anhu*) could be heard from the last rows, as it has been reported to us by 'Abdullaah ibn Shaddaad, who said: *'I heard the sobbing of 'Umar from the last rows, while he was reciting the verse from the Qur'aan:*

$$قَالَ إِنَّمَا أَشْكُواْ بَثِّي وَحُزْنِيَ إِلَى اللَّهِ$$

**I only complain of my grief and sorrow to Allaah.**[43, 44]

---

[43] Soorah Yoosuf (12):86.

[44] Reported by al-Bukhaaree in a *mu'allaq* and *jazm* form, and authenticated by our Shaykh in *al-Mukhtasar* (1/182), he says: "Sa'eed ibn Mansoor connected it with a *saheeh* chain to himself and added, 'In the morning prayer.' Ibn al-Mundhir related from another chain from 'Umar a similar narration. Al-Bayhaqee also related it (2/251) with a *saheeh* chain and it mentions that the Prayer was 'Ishaa. It seems possible that there were two incidents.

# The Weeping of 'Uthmaan ibn 'Affaan (*radiyallaahu 'anhu*)

On the authority of Haanee the freed slave of 'Uthmaan, who said: *'When 'Uthmaan ibn 'Affaan stood at a grave he would weep until his beard was wet. So it was said to him: "Indeed you make mention of Paradise and Hellfire and you do not weep, and you are weeping at this?" He replied: "Indeed the Messenger of Allaah (ﷺ) said: 'Verily the grave is the first abode of the Hereafter, if one is saved from it then what follows is made easier for him. And if one is not saved from it, then what follows is more severe.' He (ﷺ) also said: "I have never seen a sight more horrid than the grave."*[45]

---

[45] Reported by at-Tirmidhee and Ibn Maajah. At-Tirmidhee declared the *hadeeth ghareeb*. Our Shaykh said in *al-Mishkaat*: 'Its chain of narration is *hasan.*'

# The Weeping of 'Aa'ishah (*radiyallaahu 'anhaa*)

Ibn al-Haarith the nephew of 'Aa'ishah (*radiyallaahu 'anhaa*), the wife of the Prophet (ﷺ) narrated that she was told that 'Abdullaah ibn az-Zubayr (on hearing that she was selling, or giving something as a gift) said: *"By Allaah, if 'Aa'ishah does not give this up, I will make hijrah from her (i.e., boycott her)." She asked, "Did he ('Abdullaah ibn az-Zubayr) say this?" They (the people) replied, "Yes." 'Aa'ishah then said, " I vow to Allaah that I will never speak to Ibn az-Zubayr." When this desertion was prolonged, 'Abdullaah ibn az-Zubayr sought intercession with the people concerning her, but she said: "By Allaah, I will not accept the intercession of anyone on his behalf, and will not commit a sin by breaking my vow." When this state of affairs was prolonged on Ibn az-Zubayr (i.e., he felt it hard on himself), he spoke to al-Miswar bin Makhramah and 'Abdur-Rahmaan bin al-Aswad bin 'Abd Yaghooth, who were from the tribe of Banee Zuhrah, saying: "I beseech you, by Allaah, to (help) me to enter upon 'Aa'ishah, for it is unlawful for her to vow to cut off relations with me."*[46] *So al-Miswar and 'Abdur-Rahmaan went with him (and set forth) wrapping their cloaks around themselves, they went to 'Aa'ishah and asked her permission (to enter) saying, "Assalaamu 'alayki wa rahmatullaahi wa barakaatuhu! May we come in?" 'Aa'ishah responded: "Come in." They asked: "All of us?" She replied: "Yes, come in, all of you," unaware that Ibn az-Zubayr was also with them. So when they entered, Ibn az-Zubayr entered the place which screened ('Aa'ishah from the other men) and embraced 'Aa'ishah and started requesting her to excuse him, and wept. Al-Miswar and 'Abdur-Rahmaan also started urging her to speak to him and to accept his apology. They said to her: "You know what the Prophet (ﷺ) forbade regarding deserting (not speak-*

---

[46] Al-Haafidh said: 'Because he was her nephew, and she was mainly responsible for his upbringing.'

*ing to your Muslim brethren), for it is unlawful for any Muslim not to talk to his brother for more than three nights." So when they increased in reminding her (of the superiority of having good relations with kith and kin, and of excusing others' sins), and of the unhappy and unpleasant constrictions that are a consequence of breaking the ties of relationship, she started reminding them while she wept saying: "I have made a vow, and (the issue of a) vow is a difficult one." They (al-Miswar and 'Abdur-Rahmaan) persisted in their appeal until she spoke to 'Abdullaah ibn az-Zubayr and she freed forty slaves as an expiation for her vow. Later on, whenever she remembered her vow, she would weep so profusely that her veil would become wet with her tears.[47]*

---

[47] Reported by al-Bukhaaree.

# The Weeping of Umm Aiman (*radiyallaahu 'anhu*) and her Stirring Aboo Bakr and 'Umar (*radiyallaahu 'anhumaa*) to Weep

On the authority of Anas, who said: '*Aboo Bakr said to 'Umar, after the death of the Messenger of Allaah (ﷺ): "Let us go and visit Umm Aiman,*[48] *as the Messenger of Allaah (ﷺ) used to visit her." When they finished visiting her (and were about to leave) she began to cry. So they asked her: "What is it that makes you cry? Is not that which is with Allaah better for the Messenger of Allaah (ﷺ)?" So she replied,: "I am not crying because I am unaware that that which is with Allaah is better for the Messenger of Allaah (ﷺ), but I am crying because the revelation from the heavens has stopped." This moved them to tears, so they both began to weep with her.*[49]

---

[48] She (*radiyallaahu 'anhaa*) used to be the nursemaid and servant of the Messenger of Allaah (ﷺ), during his childhood.
[49] Reported by Muslim.

# The Weeping of 'Abdur-Ra<u>h</u>maan ibn 'Auf
## (ra<u>d</u>iyallaahu 'anhu)

On the authority of Sa'd ibn Ibraaheem, that his father said: *''Abdul Ra<u>h</u>maan ibn 'Auf was brought some food when he had been fasting, and he remarked: "Mu<u>s</u>'ab ibn 'Umayr, has been martyred, and he was better than me. His shroud was so short, that if his head was covered (with it) then his legs showed, and if his legs were covered, then his head showed, and I witnessed this." He also said: "<u>H</u>amzah was martyred and he was better than me. And now the world has been spread out for us." Or he said: "We have been given from the abundance of the world, and we fear that we have been rewarded for our good deeds here (quickly in this world only)." Then he began to cry, such that he left his food.''*[50]

---

[50] Reported by al-Bukhaaree.

# The Weeping of Salmaan al-Faarasee
## (*radiyallaahu 'anhu*)

On the authority of Anas (*radiyallaahu 'anhu*), who said: '*Salmaan suffering from illness, so Sa'd visited him and saw him crying, so he said to him: "What is it that makes you weep, O my brother? Did you not accompany the Messenger of Allaah (ﷺ)? Is that not so, is that not so?!" Salmaan replied: "I am not weeping for either of the following reasons: I am not weeping for the sake of the world, nor out of hate of the Hereafter. Rather, the Messenger of Allaah (ﷺ) entrusted me with a pledge, and I can only see myself as having transgressed." So he asked: "What were you entrusted with?" He replied: "He entrusted me with a pledge that the provision of a traveller should suffice anyone of us, and I see myself as only having transgressed. And as for you, O Sa'd! Fear Allaah with your ruling when you make a judgement, and fear Him with your distribution when you distribute, and fear Him with your intention when you make an intention to do something."*'[51]

Thaabit said: '*I heard that he only left twenty dirhams from the money that he had (after his death).*'[52]

---

[51]  Reported by Ibn Maajah (*Saheeh Sunan Ibn Maajah)*, and others, and it is *saheeh* . Refer to *as-Saheehah*.
[52]  From *Saheeh Sunan Ibn Maajah*.

# The Weeping of Aboo Haashim ibn 'Utbah
## (*radiyallaahu 'anhu*)

On the authority of Samurah bin Sahm, who said: '*I went to Aboo Haashim ibn 'Utbah, and he had a knife wound. So Mu'aawiyah came to visit him, and Aboo Haashim was crying. So Mu'aawiyah asked: "What is it that makes you cry, O uncle?! Is it the pain, or is it for the world (that you are crying)." He replied: "Neither, but the Messenger of Allaah (*) entrusted me with a trust, and I wish that I had carried it out." He said: "Verily you may attain some of the wealth which will divided between the people. Indeed, sufficient for you is: a servant and a riding animal for the sake of Allaah." So I did attain this wealth and accumulated it (i.e., he acquired more than what the Prophet (*) advised him to suffice himself with).*'[53]

---

[53] Reported by Ahmad, at-Tirmidhee, an-Nasaa'ee and Ibn Maajah. Our Shaykh declared it *hasan* in *at-Ta'aleeq ar-Ragheeb*.

# The Path Towards Weeping out of Fear of Allaah

• *Taqwa* of Allaah, diligently working hard to achieve it, and being sincere[54] in it

Allaah, the Most High, says in the Qur'aan:

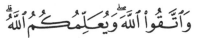

**Fear Allaah and Allaah teaches you.**[55]

It has been mentioned in *Roo_h_ al-Ma'aanee:* '**Fear Allaah**', in what he has ordered you to do and in what he has forbidden you from. And '**Allaah teaches you**' his laws, which contain your best interests. And weeping is from that.

Allaah, the Most High, says:

**As for those who strive hard in Us (our cause), We will surely guide them to our paths.**[56]

And weeping is also from that.

On the authority of Anas (*ra_d_iyallaahu 'anhu*), on the authority of the Messenger of Allaah (ﷺ), who said: *"Three types of people will find the sweetness of eemaan: the one to whom Allaah and His Messenger (ﷺ) are more beloved than anything else; the one who loves another person purely for the sake of Allaah; and the one who hates to return to disbelief, after Allaah has rescued him from it, just as he would hate to be thrown into the fire."*[57] And weeping is included in this sweetness.

---

[54] Refer to my book: *The Book of Sincerity* (al-Irshaad, 1997, Middlesbrough, U.K.).

[55] Soorah al-Baqarah (2):282.

[56] Soorah al-'Ankaboot (29):69.

[57] Reported by al-Bukhaaree and Muslim.

## • Knowledge

Allaah, the Most High, says in the Qur'aan:

$$إِنَّمَا يَخْشَى ٱللَّهَ مِنْ عِبَادِهِ ٱلْعُلَمَٰٓؤُاْ$$

**It is only those who have knowledge amongst His slaves, that fear Allaah.**[58]

Allaah, the Most High, also says in the Qur'aan:

$$أُوْلَٰٓئِكَ ٱلَّذِينَ$$
$$أَنْعَمَ ٱللَّهُ عَلَيْهِم مِّنَ ٱلنَّبِيِّـۧنَ مِن ذُرِّيَّةِ ءَادَمَ وَمِمَّنْ حَمَلْنَا مَعَ نُوحٍ$$
$$وَمِن ذُرِّيَّةِ إِبْرَٰهِيمَ وَإِسْرَٰٓءِيلَ وَمِمَّنْ هَدَيْنَا وَٱجْتَبَيْنَآ إِذَا أُنَّلَىٰ عَلَيْهِمْ$$
$$ءَايَٰتُ ٱلرَّحْمَٰنِ خَرُّواْ سُجَّدًا وَبُكِيًّا ۩ ۞ ۝ فَخَلَفَ مِنۢ بَعْدِهِمْ$$
$$خَلْفٌ أَضَاعُواْ ٱلصَّلَوٰةَ وَٱتَّبَعُواْ ٱلشَّهَوَٰتِ فَسَوْفَ يَلْقَوْنَ غَيًّا$$
$$۝ إِلَّا مَن تَابَ وَءَامَنَ وَعَمِلَ صَٰلِحًا فَأُوْلَٰٓئِكَ يَدْخُلُونَ ٱلْجَنَّةَ$$
$$وَلَا يُظْلَمُونَ شَيْـًٔا ۝$$

**They were those unto whom Allaah bestowed His Grace from among the Prophets, of the offspring of Aadam and of those whom We carried (In the ship) with Noo<u>h</u>, and of the offspring of Ibraaheem and Israa'eel - and from amongst those whom We guided and chose. When the verses of the Most Gracious were recited to them, they fell down prostrating and weeping. Then there has succeeded them a poster-**

---

58    Soorah al-Faa<u>t</u>ir (35):28.

ity who have given up the Prayer (*as-Salaah*), and have followed lusts. So they will be thrown in Hell. Except those who repent and believe, and work righteousness. Such will enter Paradise, and they will not be wronged in ought.[59]

Allaah, the Most High, says:

Say: Believe in it (i.e., the Qur'aan) or do not believe (in it). Verily! those who were given knowledge before it, when it is recited to them, fall down on their faces in humble prostration, and they say: "Glory be to our Lord! Truly the promise of our Lord must be fulfilled. And they fall down on their faces weeping, and it adds to their humility.[60]

'Abdul A'laa al-Taymee, said with regard to these noble verses: *"Whoever is given knowledge that doesn't make him weep, then clearly he has not been given knowledge that benefits, because Allaah, the Most High, has described the knowledgeable by saying:*

---

59  Soorah Maryam (19):58-60.
60  Soorah al-Israa' (17):107-109.

35

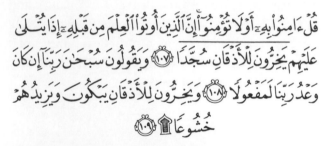

قُلْ ءَامِنُوا بِهِ أَوْ لَا تُؤْمِنُوا إِنَّ الَّذِينَ أُوتُوا الْعِلْمَ مِن قَبْلِهِ إِذَا يُتْلَىٰ
عَلَيْهِمْ يَخِرُّونَ لِلْأَذْقَانِ سُجَّدًا ۝ وَيَقُولُونَ سُبْحَانَ رَبِّنَا إِن كَانَ
وَعْدُ رَبِّنَا لَمَفْعُولًا ۝ وَيَخِرُّونَ لِلْأَذْقَانِ يَبْكُونَ وَيَزِيدُهُمْ
خُشُوعًا ۝

**Say: Believe in it (i.e., the Qur'aan) or do not believe (in it). Verily! those who were given knowledge before it, when it is recited to them, fall down on their faces in humble prostration, and they say: "Glory be to our Lord! Truly the promise of our Lord must be fulfilled. And they fall down on their faces weeping, and it adds to their humility."**[61]

Allaah, the Most High, says in the Qur'aan:

وَلِيَعْلَمَ الَّذِينَ أُوتُوا الْعِلْمَ أَنَّهُ الْحَقُّ مِن رَّبِّكَ فَيُؤْمِنُوا بِهِ
فَتُخْبِتَ لَهُ قُلُوبُهُمْ وَإِنَّ اللَّهَ لَهَادِ الَّذِينَ ءَامَنُوا إِلَىٰ صِرَاطٍ مُّسْتَقِيمٍ

**And those who have been given knowledge know that it (the Qur'aan) is the truth from your Lord, and that they may believe therein, and their hearts may submit to it with humility. And verily Allaah is the Guide of those who believe in the Straight Path.**[62]

On the authority of Aboo Dharr (*radiyallaahu 'anhu*), who said that the Messenger of Allaah (ﷺ) said: *"I can see what you do not see,*

---

61  Soorah Al-Israa' (17):107-109.
62  Soorah al-Hajj (22):54.

*and I can hear what you do not hear. Indeed the sky groans[63] and it has a right to do so. There is not an area equal to that of four fingers, except that an angel is prostrating to Allaah therein. By Allaah! If you knew what I know you would laugh little and weep much, and you would not enjoy your wives in bed. But rather you would come out onto the hills, supplicating and praying fervently to Allaah."[64]*

## • The Remembrance of Death

There is no doubt that death ends the delights and pleasures of this life, just as the Messenger of Allaah (ﷺ) has told us: *"Increase in your remembrance of the destroyer of all pleasures:[65] i.e., death. For verily, one who remembers it when enduring the hardships of life, it widens it for him (i.e., he no longer feels overburdened with the hardships he is experiencing). Whenever one remembers it at times of opulence, it will cause him to feel restricted and burdened (i.e., he will not then be too involved with this life and will start to reflect on the serious and heavy matters awaiting him)."[66]*

The pleasures are what prevent a tear to be shed, nor any sadness and grief to be felt in the heart. So increase in your remembrance of death, in an attempt to feel the terrors and horrors that will follow it, fearing an evil destination, so that you may succeed with weeping out of fear of Allaah. Indeed this is easy for the one whom Allaah wishes to make it easy for.

---

[63] The large numbers of angels in the sky make it heavy so that it groans.

[64] Reported by Ahmad, at-Tirmidhee, Ibn Maajah and others. It is *hasan*. Our Shaykh reported it in *as-Saheehah*. Reported by al-Bukhaaree in summarised form with the words: *"If you knew what I know, you would laugh little and weep much,"* just as our Shaykh indicated in the mentioned sources.

[65] Refer to *Fayd al-Qadeer*.

[66] Reported by an-Nasaa'ee, at-Tirmidhee, Ibn Maajah and others. Tirmidhee said it is *hasan ghareeb*. Our Shaykh however said: 'It is *saheeh*, and there are many witnesses...' Also reported by Ibn Hibbaan, al-Haakim and others.

On the authority of Ibn 'Umar (*radiyallaahu 'anhumaa*) who said: *'I was with the Messenger of Allaah (ﷺ) when a man from the Ansaar came up to the Messenger of Allaah (ﷺ) and greeted him with the salaam and then said: "O Messenger of Allaah (ﷺ) which of the believers are the best?" He replied: "Those who are best in character." Then he asked: "Which of the believers are the most intelligent?" He (ﷺ) replied: "Those who remember death the most, and those who are best prepared for what comes after it (death). These are the intelligent ones."*[67]

## • Contemplating and Reflecting over the Terrors which Follow Death

Contemplation and reflection upon death makes one fear the terrors and horrors which follow, beginning with the terrors of the grave and the *barzakh*[68] (the transitional period in the grave before the Day of Judgement). Do not think that death is far off, since the Messenger of Allaah (ﷺ) has warned us from thinking in this way. He (ﷺ) said: *"Paradise is closer to any one of you than your shoe lace as is the Hellfire."* [69] There are many texts concerning this, and I will be mentioning a few of them as exhortation and remembrance.

On the authority of Aboo Hurayrah (*radiyallaahu 'anhu*) who said: *'We were sitting with the Messenger of Allaah (ﷺ) when we heard a loud thud. The Messenger of Allaah (ﷺ) asked: "Do you know what that was?" We replied: "Allaah and His Messenger (ﷺ) know best." He then told us: "That was a stone which was thrown into the Hellfire seventy years ago, it was sinking further into the Fire and has just reached the bottom."*[70]

---

[67] Declared *hasan* by our Shaykh in *as-Saheehah* by virtue of all its different chains of narration.

[68] Refer to my book: *The Grave, Punishments and Blessings* (Ibn Hazm Publishing House, 1997, Beirut, Lebanan).

[69] Reported by al-Bukhaaree.

[70] Reported by Muslim.

The Messenger of Allaah (ﷺ) said: *"Verily the eyes of the Companion of the horn,*[71] *ever since he was appointed with it, are fixed, gazing towards the Throne (of Allaah, not looking away) fearing that he will be ordered to blow the horn before his eyes fall back on the throne, and his eyes are like two brilliant stars."*[72]

In another narration: *"How can I lead a life of ease when the angel of the horn has put it to his lips and raised his forehead anticipating to hear the call, so when he is ordered to blow he will blow." So the Muslims said: "What should we say (supplicate) O Messenger of Allaah (ﷺ)?" He replied: "Say: Sufficient is Allaah for us and He is the best of Guardians, we put our trust in Allaah, our Lord" – and perhaps Sufyaan said: 'upon Allaah we put our trust.'*[73]

How could he (the Prophet (ﷺ)) take pleasure and he had the lawful things in mind! How is it then, for the one who commits offences and sins, while the angel of the horn has already put the horn to his lips, anticipating to hear the call, such that when he is ordered, he will blow.

On the authority of Anas ibn Maalik (*radiyallaahu 'anhu*) who related that the Messenger of Allaah (ﷺ) said: *"Weeping will be sent to he inhabitants of the Hellfire whereby they will be made to weep until their tears have been used up, then they will weep tears of*

---

[71] The horn which is blown into (when the Day of Judgement is to be established). It is reported like this by Ibn al-Mubaarak in *az-Zuhd*, and by at-Tirmidhee, Aboo Daawood and others. It is a *saheeh hadeeth* which our Shaykh reported in *as-Saheehah*.

[72] Reported by al-Haakim and others. It is *saheeh*, our Shaykh reported it in *as-Saheehah*.

[73] Our Shaykh reported it in *as-Saheehah*.

*blood until it (the blood) leaves trenches in their faces, and if ships were placed therein, they would sail."*[74]

In another narration (the Messenger of Allaah (ﷺ) said): *"O people weep! And if you can not weep then make yourself weep, for indeed the inhabitants of the Hellfire will weep until their tears pour down their cheeks, as if they were streams, until the tears dry up. Then blood will flow and the eyes will be covered with ulcers."*[75]

On the authority of 'Abdullaah ibn 'Amr (*radiyallaahu 'anhu*), that the Messenger of Allaah (ﷺ) said: *"Indeed the inhabitants of the Hellfire will call upon Maalik (an angel), and he will not answer (their call), for forty years, and then he will say: 'Verily you are dwellers here.' Then they will call upon their Lord, saying: 'O our Lord, take us out from here, for if we return (to committing sins), then verily we are transgressors.' Allaah will not respond to their call for a span equivalent to the time span of this world, and then the Most High will say: 'Away with them to the Hellfire, and do not speak.' Then the people will give up all hope and there will only be (the sound) of moaning, sobbing and braying. Their voices will be similar to the sound of donkeys, the first of them braying and the last of them moaning."*[76]

On the authority of Aboo Dardaa (*radiyallaahu 'anhu*) who related that the Messenger of Allaah (ﷺ) said: *"Verily in front of you (all)*

---

[74] Reported by Ibn Maajah, our Shaykh declared it *hasan* in *Saheeh at-Targheeb wat Tarheeb*. Refer to *as-Saheehah*.

[75] Our Shaykh declared it *hasan* in *Saheeh at-Targheeb wat Tarheeb*.

[76] Al-Mundhiree said in *at-Targheeb wat-Tarheeb:* Reported by at-Tabraanee in *mawqoof* form. Our Shaykh declared it *saheeh* in *at-Ta'leeq ar-Ragheeb*, where he mentions some important points concerning this *hadeeth*.

*is an insurmountable obstacle, which will not be surmounted by those overburdened."*[77] In another wording by Umm Dardaa, on the authority of Aboo Dardaa, she said: '*I asked him (Aboo Dardaa), "What is it with you, you do not ask for that which such and such a person asks for?"' He replied: 'Verily I heard the Messenger of Allaah (ﷺ) say: "Indeed behind you is a insurmountable obstacle, which those with a heavy burden will not be able to pass.' So indeed I wish to lighten my load in preparation for that obstacle."*[78]

Therefore, in order to remember death and contemplate over the horrors which follow death, one must:

## • Visit the Graves

The Messenger of Allaah (ﷺ) said: *"I had forbidden you from visiting the graves (before), but now you should visit them."*[79] In another narration, he (ﷺ) said: *"Visit the graves for verily it is a reminder of death."*[80] In another narration he (ﷺ) said: *"Visiting (the graves) will increase you in good."*[81]

In a narration of Aboo Sa'eed al-Khudree (*radiyallaahu 'anhu*), who said that the Messenger of Allaah (ﷺ) said: *"Indeed! I had forbid-*

---

[77] Al-Mundharee said in *at-Targheeb wat-Tarheeeb:* Al-Bazzaar reported it with a *hasan* chain of narration. Our Shaykh declared it *saheeh* in *Saheeh at-Targheeb wat-Tarheeb.*

[78] Reported by at-Tabraanee with a *saheeh* chain of narration, just as al-Mundhiree has stated in *at-Targheeb wat-Tarheeb.* Our Shaykh declared it *saheeh* in *Saheeh at-Targheeb wat-Tarheeb.*

[79] Reported by Muslim.

[80] Reported by Muslim.

[81] Reported by Ahmad. It is a *saheeh hadeeth* that our Shaykh has related in *Ahkaam ul-Janaa'iz.*

*den you from visiting the graves (before), but now you should visit them, for verily there is a lesson and an admonition in this."*[82]

In a narration by Anas bin Maalik (*radiyallaahu 'anhu*), who said that the Messenger of Allaah (ﷺ) said: *"I used to forbid you from visiting the graves, but now you should visit them, for indeed the hearts are softened, the eyes are made to shed tears, and it is a remembrance of the hereafter."*[83]

## • Make the Hereafter your Main Concern

'Abdur-Rahmaan ibn 'Uthmaan ibn 'Affaan (*radiyallaahu 'anhu*) reported from his father, who said: *'Zayd ibn Thaabit left Marwaan at midday. I said: "Nothing made him (i.e. Marwaan) send for him at this hour, except that he wanted to ask about something." I asked him (about this), so he replied: 'We were asked about things which we had heard from the Messenger of Allaah (ﷺ), I had heard the Messenger of Allaah (ﷺ) say: "Whoever sets this world as his goal, Allaah divides his affairs for him, He will place poverty between his eyes, and nothing will come to him from the world except what Allaah has written for him. Whoever sets the Hereafter as his goal, Allaah gathers his affairs for him, gives him richness of the heart and the world will come to him grudgingly and submissivley" "*[84]

On the authority of 'Abdullaah, who related that he heard the Messenger of Allaah (ﷺ) say: *"Whoever makes the Hereafter his sole*

---

[82] Reported by Ahmad and al-Haakim, who declared it *saheeh* upon the conditions of Muslim, adh-Dhahabee agreed with him as did our Shaykh in *Ahkaam ul-Janaa'iz*.

[83] Reported by al-Haakim and others, it is declared *saheeh* by our Shaykh in *Ahkaam ul-Janaa'iz*.

[84] Reported by Ibn Maajah and Ibn Hibbaan. Authenticated by our Shaykh in *as-Saheehah*.

*concern, then Allaah will be sufficient for him concerning his affairs and needs in the world, and whoever's concerns (in the world) are divided amongst the affairs of the world, then Allaah would have no care in which path he is destroyed."*[85]

On the authority of Aboo Hurayrah (*radiyallaahu 'anhu*) who said, that the Messenger of Allaah (ﷺ) said: *"Allaah says: O Son of Aadam, devote yourself to worshipping Me, and I will fill your bosom with richness and remove your poverty. And if you do not do this, then I will fill your bosom with occupation and distraction and I will not remove your poverty."*[86]

## • Reflecting upon the Magnificent Qur'aan

Allaah, the Most High, says in the Qur'aan:

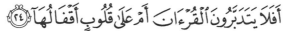

**Do they not then think deeply in the Qur'aan, or
are their hearts locked up (from understanding it)!**[87]

Contemplating over the Qur'aan is one of the strongest ways of reaching the state of weeping. It is necessary for one to take particular interest over the *tafseer* (explanation) of the Qur'aan, in continuously seek help from the scholars and the people of *tafseer* as much as one can. Read the Qur'aan as if it was revealed to you, as some of the scholars have said.

An example of this has been established by 'Aa'ishah (*radiyallaahu 'anhaa*), when she said: '*A man sat in front of the Messenger of Allaah (ﷺ) and said: "O Messenger of Allaah (ﷺ) verily I have*

---

[85] Reported by Ibn Maajah and others. Authenticated by our Shaykh in *al-Mishkaat*.

[86] Reported by at-Tirmidhee, Ibn Maajah and Ibn Ḥibbaan and others. It is a *saheeh hadeeth* and related by our Shaykh in *as-Saheehah*.

[87] Soorah Muḥammad (47):24.

*slaves, they lie to me, are disloyal to me and disobey me. When I came to know about this I scold them and beat them. So tell me, how have I been with them?"* The Messenger of Allaah (ﷺ) replied: *"What they were disloyal to you about, what they disobeyed you in, and what they lied to you about is measured, and the punishment which you inflicted upon them is also measured. If your punishment was equal to their sins, then the scale of balance is equal, it is not for you and nor is it against you. If your punishment to them was not to the extent of their sins (i.e. less than they deserved) then that is for you (i.e., in your favour). However if your punishment ex-ceeded their sins (i.e. more than they deserved) then that is against you."* The man then fell back and began to weep and scream. The Messenger of Allaah (ﷺ) said: *"Haven't you read the verse in the Book of Allaah:*

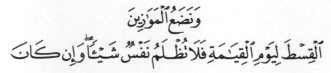

**...and we shall set up balances on the Day of Resur-rection, then none will be dealt with unjustly in any-thing...** [88]

*The man replied: "By Allaah, O Messenger of Allaah (ﷺ) I do not see anything better for me and them than they leave me, I call you to witness that all of them are free."* [89]

Ibn 'Uyaynah said: *'When Mu<u>h</u>ammad ibn al-Munkadir was close to death, he became anxious and worried, so they called Aboo <u>H</u>aazim for him. When he arrived Ibn al-Munkadir said to him: "Indeed Allaah says:*

---

[88] Soorah al-Ambiyaa' (21):47.

[89] Reported in *Sa<u>h</u>ee<u>h</u> Sunan at-Tirmidhee* and our Shaykh declared it *<u>s</u>ahee<u>h</u>* in *Sa<u>h</u>ee<u>h</u> at-Targheeb wat-Tarheeb*.

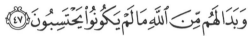

**...it will become clear to them, from Allaah, what they were not anticipating.**[90]

*And I am afraid that that which I am not anticipating will appear in front of me." Upon this they both began to weep.*[91]

## • Being Concerned with Listening to the Humble and Effective Recitation of the Qur'aan and Reading More of the Heart Softening Books[92]

Verily this has a great effect in driving away the *Shaytaan*, softening the heart and shedding tears.

It has been reported that a man complained to Hasan about the hardness of his heart. So he said: "Bring it closer to the remembrance of Allaah, and he also said: The gatherings of *dhikr* (remembering Allaah) give life to knowledge and bring about *khushoo'* in the heart. The dead heart is brought to life with the remembrance of Allaah, just as the dead earth is brought to life with rain."[93]

---

90 Soorah az-Zumar (39):47.

91 Reported by Ibn Aboo Haatim and Ibn Abee ad-Dunyaa added: 'His (al-Munkadir's) family said to him (Aboo Haazim): "We called you to relieve him of his worry and anxicty but you have increased it," so he informed them of what he (al-Munkadir) had said to him.'

92 Amongst these books are: *Az-Zuhd* by Ibn al-Mubaarak; *Az-Zuhd* by Imaam Ahmad; *At-Tuhfah tul-'Iraaqiyyah fil A'amaal il-Qalbiyyah* by Shaykh al-Islaam Ibn Taymiyyah; the works of Ibn Qayyim al-Jawziyyah; *Tahdheeb Mawi'dhatil-Mu'mineen min Ihyaa 'Uloom id-Deen* by al-Qaasimee; the books of the Shaykh 'Abdul 'Azeez as-Salmaan; and the books of Muhammad Saalih al-Munajjad on this topic.

93 For an excellent discussion refer to the section, "The Excellence of the Gatherings of *Dhikr* and Admonition" in *Lataa'if al-Ma'aarif*.

## • Seeking Forgiveness and Taking Account of Oneself

There is no doubt that seeking forgiveness (from Allaah) has a great effect in purifying and polishing the heart. As well as increasing the soul in strength and firmness. The more truthful a person is in seeking forgiveness, the more *khushoo'* one feels, and the more one's heart softens.

To increase in seeking Allaah's forgiveness - just as it was the practice of the Messenger of Allaah (ﷺ)[94] - it is necessary to take account of oneself and remember one's sins, as Allaah says in the Qur'aan:

يَـٰٓأَيُّهَا ٱلَّذِينَ ءَامَنُوا۟ ٱتَّقُوا۟ ٱللَّهَ وَلْتَنظُرْ نَفْسٌ مَّا قَدَّمَتْ لِغَدٍ

**O you who believe, fear Allaah and keep your duty to Him. And let every person look to what he has sent forth for tomorrow.**[95]

Allaah has ordered us to take account of ourselves, perform righteous actions and prepare for the Day of Gathering. Allaah, the Most High, says in the Qur'aan:

لَآ أُقْسِمُ بِيَوْمِ ٱلْقِيَـٰمَةِ ۝ وَلَآ أُقْسِمُ بِٱلنَّفْسِ ٱللَّوَّامَةِ ۝

---

[94] From the proofs of this is his (ﷺ) saying: *"By Allaah I seek forgiveness from Allaah and repent to Him more than seventy times a day."* Reported by al-Bukhaaree. Also his (ﷺ) saying: *"Verily my heart becomes preoccupied and verily I seek Allaah's forgiveness a hundred times a day."* The reference is to 'the forgetfulness' that overcomes him which befalls all people. The Prophet's heart was always occupied with Allaah, the Most High, if at some time a normal and human state befalls him that is accidental, which preoccupies him from matters of the *ummah*, religion and its welfare, he would regard it as a sin and would race to seek forgiveness from Allaah (*An-Nihaayah*).
[95] Soorah al-Hashr (59):18.

**I swear by the Day of Resurrection and the self-reproaching soul.**[96]

'Ikrimah said in an explanation of this noble verse: *'It is to blame oneself in good and evil, whether you have done that or not.'* Sa'eed Ibn Jubayr said: *'It is to blame oneself when doing good and evil.'* Mujaahid said: *'To regret for what has passed, and blame oneself for it.'*[97]

'Abdullaah Ibn Ma'sood (*radiyallaahu 'anhumaa*) said: *'Verily the believer sees his sins as if he is standing under a mountain, afraid that it will collapse upon him. And verily the evildoer sees his sins as flies passing by his nose and he does this to it.'* Aboo Shihaab[98] said (while clarifying the action that Ibn Mas'ood made when he said "*he does this to it*"): *'He moves it (the fly) away by swiping his hand over his nose.'*[99]

It is reported that 'Umar ibn al-Khattaab (*radiyallaahu 'anhu*) said: *'Bring yourselves to account before you are brought to account, and weigh your deeds before they are weighed.'*[100]

It is reported that Maymoon ibn Mihraan said: *'A slave is not from among the muttaqeen (those who fear Allaah), until he brings him-*

---

[96] Soorah al-Qiyaamah (75):1-2.

[97] Refer to *Tafseer Ibn Katheer.*

**Translators note:** *Nafs al-lawaamah*: the self-reproaching soul - comes from the Arabic root word *laam* or *lawm* which means: to blame one's self or others and criticise sharply. Thus when Allaah swears by the self-reproaching soul, the meaning includes the one who scrutinises his actions and criticises himself severely.

[98] Aboo Shihaab is one of the narrators of this narration.

[99] Reported by al-Bukhaaree.

[100] Mentioned by at-Tirmidhee in a *tamreedh* form, see *Tuhfat al-Ahwadhee - hadeeth* no. 2577.

*self to account more severely and thoroughly than keeping account of his business partner, the two partners bring themselves to account after every action.*'[101]

Furthermore: *'the believer is firm in bringing himself to account for (the sake of) Allaah. Indeed lighter is the reckoning of a person who brings himself to account in the world; and indeed difficult is the reckoning on the Day of Judgement for a people who did not bring themselves to account (in the world).*'[102]

Beware of the minor sins, as the Messenger of Allaah (ﷺ) has said: *"Beware of minor sins, verily the example of those who commit minor sins is like a group of people who descended upon a valley. One of them brought a stick, and then another person brought a stick, and then another and another, until they gathered enough for (a fire), to cook their bread. This is similar to the idea of minor sins, because the accumulation of small sins will eventually become enough to destroy you (just like the piling of sticks was eventually enough to create a fire)."*[103]

## • Perfecting the Prayer[104]

It was reported by Aboo Ayyoob, who said: *'A man came to the Messenger of Allaah (ﷺ) and said: "Teach me in the briefest words" He (ﷺ) replied: "When you stand in prayer, pray as if you are bidding farewell (to this world), and do not utter words for which you*

---

[101] Mentioned by at-Tirmidhee also in a *tamreedh* form, see *Tuhfat al-Ahwadhee - hadeeth* no. 2577.

[102] Attributed to Hasan. It's meaning is *saheeh*.

[103] Reported by Ahmad and others. It is *saheeh* and our Shaykh authenticated it in *as-Saheehah*.

[104] Refer to my book: *The Prayer - its Effects in Increasing Eemaan and Purifying the Soul* (al-Hidaayah Publishing and Distribution, 1995, Birmingham, U.K.).

*will have to seek an excuse, and do not wish for that which the people have."*,[105]

What an excellent prayer is the prayer of one who prays as if he is leaving the world and its beauties, and in which one remembers death, thereby softening the heart and causing the eyes to weep.

## • Making Yourself Weep[106]

So know, may Allaah have mercy upon you, that making yourself weep earns less of a reward than actually weeping. However it is the way towards weeping, that is because the one who makes himself weep, is among those who strive hard and fight their souls, and take account of themselves, and endeavour to attain the pleasure of Allaah the Most High. Allaah says:

$$ وَٱلَّذِينَ جَٰهَدُواْ فِينَا لَنَهۡدِيَنَّهُمۡ سُبُلَنَا $$

**And those who strive hard in Us (i.e., our cause), We will surely guide them to our paths.**[107]

---

[105] Reported by Ibn Maajah, Aḥmad and Aboo Nu'aym in *al-Ḥilyah*. It is a *hasan hadeeth* which our Shaykh has related in *as-Saheehah*.

[106] After speaking about the types of weeping, Ibn al-Qayyim discusses those who urge themselves to weep; he says in *Zaad al-Ma'aad*: 'This can be of two types: praiseworthy or blameworthy. As for the praiseworthy type of weeping, then it is sought after to soften the heart and to increase one's deep fear of Allaah, and it is not for the sake of being heard or seen by the people. As for the blameworthy type of weeping, it is sought after because of the creation... The statement of 'Umar (*raḍiyallaahu 'anhu*) is mentioned with regards to the prisoners of war from the battle of Badr: '...and if I do not cry, then I will make myself cry, because you are both crying.' The Prophet (ﷺ) did not disapprove of it. Some of the *salaf* have said, "Weep out of the deep fear of Allaah and if you cannot weep then make yourself weep."'

[107] Soorah al-'Ankaboot (29):69.

So whoever strives to make his soul weep, then Allaah will guide this person to sincere weeping and give him success in achieving it.

On the authority of Anas (*radiyallaahu 'anhu*), who related that he heard the Messenger of Allaah (ﷺ) say, *"O people weep, for if you cannot weep then make yourself weep. Indeed the inhabitants of the Hellfire will weep until their tears pour down  their cheeks, as if they were streams until the tears are used up and (then) blood will pour down, and the eyes will be covered with ulcers."*[108]

So reflect over the way the Messenger of Allaah (ﷺ) ordered us to weep or to make ourselves weep. He (ﷺ) (also) explained the weeping of the inhabitants of the Hellfire i.e., the tears will pour down their cheeks and faces as if streams until the tears are used up, after which blood will pour forth and cause the eyes to be wounded with ulcers.

What else can you want after this, O slave of Allaah, in order for you to weep! For I swear by Allaah that it is a deep and serious admonition, this admonition is enough for you to cause you to make *tawbah* (repent to Allaah), return to Allaah and weep. For are you really safe from the scene (described above)?!

Are you guaranteed salvation and Paradise? So weep and shed tears now for which you will be rewarded in your (life of the) world, before you weep blood, for which you will not be rewarded in the Hereafter.

If you do not weep or even try to weep, then know that your *eemaan* (faith) is weak and the world has overtaken you, and you are in great danger. So flee to Allaah, grab hold of life before death and

---

[108] Declared *hasan* by our Shaykh in *Saheeh at-Targheeb wat-Tarheeb.*

rush to sincere repentance, true *inaabah* (returning to Allaah) and righteous actions.

On the authority of Ibn Abee Mulaykah, who said: *'We were sitting with 'Abdullaah ibn 'Amr (radiyallaahu 'anhu) on a rock. He said, "Weep and if you cannot weep, then make yourself weep. If only you knew, you would pray until your back broke and weep until you lost your voice."*'[109]

In the story of the prisoners of *Badr*, Ibn 'Abbaas (*radiyallaahu 'anhumaa*) said: 'When the prisoners (of *Badr*) were chained, the Messenger of Allaah (ﷺ) asked Aboo Bakr and 'Umar (*radiyallaahu 'anhumaa*), *"What should be done with the prisoners?"* Aboo Bakr said *"O Prophet of Allaah! They are our relatives, I think that you should take ransom from them and it will be a power for us against the disbelievers. Maybe Allaah will guide them to Islaam."* The Messenger of Allaah then asked, *"What do you think O son of al-Khattaab?"* I ('Umar) said, *"No, I swear by Allaah, I do not agree with Aboo Bakr's view. I think that you should let us strike their necks. So let 'Alee kill 'Aqeel, and let me kill such and such a person (a relative of 'Umar). Verily they are the leaders and notables of disbelief."* The Messenger of Allaah (ﷺ) approved of what Aboo Bakr had said as opposed to what I had said. So, the following day, when I came, I found the Messenger of Allaah (ﷺ) and Aboo Bakr (*radiyallaahu 'anhu*) sitting (together) and weeping, I said: *"O Messenger of Allaah (ﷺ)! Inform me of the thing, which is making*

---

[109] He said in *Targheeb wat-Tarheeb*: "al-Haakim reported it in *marfoo'* form and said: It is *saheeh* upon their condition." Our Shaykh said in *al-Ta'leeq ar-Ragheeb*: "It is clear that it is a misprint, and the context alludes to this, just as in *al-Mustadrak*. Adh-Dhahabee agrees upon its authenticity and it is as he has said. It is reported by Ibn al-Mubaarak in *mawqoof* form in *az-Zuhd*.

*you and your companion weep? If I find that it is something that*
*makes me weep, then I will weep, and if it does not make me weep,*
*then I will make myself weep, due to the weeping of both of you." So*
*the Prophet (ﷺ) said "I weep over what your companions suggested*
*with regards to taking the ransom, for their punishment has been*
*shown to me, from closer than this tree." Allaah has revealed in the*
*Qur'aan:*

$$\text{مَا كَانَ لِنَبِيٍّ أَن يَكُونَ}$$
$$\text{لَهُ أَسْرَىٰ حَتَّىٰ يُثْخِنَ فِي ٱلْأَرْضِ تُرِيدُونَ عَرَضَ ٱلدُّنْيَا}$$
$$\text{وَٱللَّهُ يُرِيدُ ٱلْأَخِرَةَ وَٱللَّهُ عَزِيزٌ حَكِيمٌ ﴿٦٧﴾ لَّوْلَا كِتَٰبٌ مِّنَ}$$
$$\text{ٱللَّهِ سَبَقَ لَمَسَّكُمْ فِيمَا أَخَذْتُمْ عَذَابٌ عَظِيمٌ ﴿٦٨﴾ فَكُلُوا مِمَّا}$$
$$\text{غَنِمْتُمْ حَلَٰلًا طَيِّبًا وَٱتَّقُوا ٱللَّهَ إِنَّ ٱللَّهَ غَفُورٌ رَّحِيمٌ ﴿٦٩﴾}$$

**It is not for the Prophet that he should have prison-
ers of war (and free them with ransom) until he had
made a great slaughter (among his enemies) in the
land.[110] You desire the good of this world (i.e., the
money of ransom for freeing the captives), but
Allaah desires (for you) the Hereafter. And Allaah
is All-Mighty, All-Wise. Were it not for a previous
ordainment from Allaah, a severe torment would
have touched you for what you took. So enjoy the**

---

[110] 'Until he had made great slaughter in the land' means, to increase in the
killing and destruction of the enemy. He said in *an-Nihaayah*: 'To massacre, is to
do this excessively, and what is meant here is, be excessive in killing the disbelievers.'

**booty you have got from war, lawful and good, and be afraid of Allaah. Certainly, Allaah is Oft-Forgiving, Most Merciful.**[111]

*So Allaah made the booty lawful for them.'*[112]

## • Taking Heed of Admonition

There are many texts with regards to this, amongst them is the *hadeeth* of al-'Irbaad ibn Saariyah (*radiyallaahu 'anhu*) which has already preceded who said: "The Messenger of Allaah (ﷺ) gave us a sermon which made our hearts tremble and our eyes flow with tears..."

The statement of Ibn 'Abbaas in explaining the following *Aayah* of the Qur'aan has also preceded:

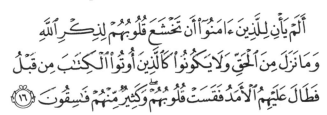

**Has not the time come for the hearts of those who believe to be affected by Allaah's reminder (this Qur'aan), and the truth which has been revealed, lest they become as those who received the scriptures before (i.e., Jews and the Christians) and the term was prolonged for them and so their hearts were hardened. And many of them were *faasiqoon* (rebellious and disobedient).**[113]

---

111    Soorah al-Anfaal (8):67-69.

112    Taken from *Saheeh Muslim*.

113    Soorah al-Hadeed (57):16.

Ibn 'Abbaas said that they are from among those people who are inclined towards the world and turn away from the admonition of Allaah. It is mentioned in *Lataa'if al-Ma'aarif* that admonition is like a whip which strikes and affects the heart just as whipping would affect the body. After the striking has stopped, the effect will cease to be the same as it was whilst one was being struck. However the effect of the pain depends on the force with which one was struck. So whenever one is struck with great force, the pain evidently remains for a longer period of time.

Many of the *Salaf*, having heard an admonition in a gathering, would leave and a sense of peace, tranquillity and dignity would descend upon them, some of them unable to eat food after that, while others would act according to what they had heard for a period of time.

When al-Hasan used to go out to the people, he was like a man who could see the Hereafter with his own eyes, and then inform others about it. And the people would leave his company considering the world to be worthless.

Sufyaan at-Thawree used to find solace from the world in his gatherings.

Ahmad was such that the world was not to be mentioned in his gatherings nor in his presence.

Some of them (the *Salaf*) said: "Admonition *is only beneficial when it comes from the heart, so indeed it reaches the heart. As for the admonition which comes from the tongue, then verily it enters through one ear and comes out from the other.*"

## • Purifying the Heart from the Dirt and Filth of Hatred, Envy and Deceit[114]

Indeed this matter has a great influence on bringing about weeping and its opposite hinders and prevents it.

## • Increase in the Voluntary Acts of Worship (*Nawaafil*)

On the authority of Aboo Hurayrah (*radiyallaahu 'anhu*), who said that he heard the Messenger of Allaah (ﷺ) say: "*Allaah has said: 'I will declare war against him who shows hostility to a pious worshipper of Mine. The most beloved things with which My slave draws closer to Me, is what I have obligated upon him; and My slave keeps drawing closer to Me through performing supererogatory acts (nawaafil) till I love him, then I become his sense of hearing with which he hears, and his sense of sight with which he sees, and his hand with which he grasps, and his leg with which he walks; and if he asks Me, I will give him; if he asks my protection (refuge), I will protect him; and I do not hesitate to do anything as I hesitate to take the soul of a believer, for he hates death and I hate to disappoint him.'*"[115]

So increase your voluntary acts of worship as much as you can in this way. Increase in your prayer, fasting, giving of *zakah*, *Hajj* and every good and righteous action as much as you are able to, so that Allaah, the Most High, may love you and grant you what you ask Him for, and from the first of these things that you ask for is that He, the Most High blesses you with the ability to weep out of deep fear of Him.

---

[114] Refer to my book *Mim Mawaaqif as-Sahaabah*, "Number 8: The Story of 'Abdullaah ibn 'Umar and a Person from Paradise."

[115] Reported by al-Bukhaaree and others.

## • Considering the World to be Worthless and Insignificant and Renouncing it

Indeed the love of this world is a reason behind the hardening of the heart and it diverts one away from the way of Allaah. Verily, abstention and renunciation of this world causes the heart to soften, increases its *khushoo'* (submission and humility) and causes the eyes to weep tearfully.

So beware of becoming too much at ease with the world. You must renounce this world and consider it insignificant as much as you can in this way, and read books which urge you to do this.[116]

Contemplate the guidance of the Prophet (ﷺ) when renouncing the world, ponder over his difficult and tough lifestyle with regards to his food, drink, clothing, furniture etc.

It is reported by 'Aa'ishah (*radiyallaahu 'anhaa*) that: *'The family of Muhammad (ﷺ), since their arrival in Madeenah, had not eaten wheat bread to their satisfaction for three consecutive nights until the Prophet (ﷺ) passed away.'*[117]

On the authority of Aboo Hurayrah (*radiyallaahu 'anhu*) who said, *'The Prophet (ﷺ) left the world (i.e. passed away) and he had not eaten barley bread to his fill.'*[118]

On the authority of 'Aa'ishah (*radiyallaahu 'anhaa*) who said that, *'The family of Muhammad (ﷺ) had not eaten barley bread to their fill for two consecutive days until the Prophet (ﷺ) passed away.'*[119]

---

[116] With regards to this subject refer to chapters 54 and 55 of *Riyaadus Saaliheen*.
[117] Reported by al-Bukhaaree and Muslim.
[118] Reported by al-Bukhaaree.
[119] Reported by Muslim.

On the authority of 'Urwah that 'Aa'ishah *(radiyallaahu 'anhaa)* said to him: *"O my nephew. We used to see three new moons in the space of two months and fire was not kindled in the houses of Allaah's Messenger (ﷺ)." So I ('Urwah) asked, "What was your means of sustenance?" She replied, "The two black things: dates and water. However Allaah's Messenger (ﷺ) had some Ansaar as neighbours who had animals, which gave milk, and they used to send some of the milk to Allaah's Messenger (ﷺ), which he served us with."* [120]

On the authority of Anas *(radiyallaahu 'anhu)* who said: *'I never knew the Prophet (ﷺ) to have eaten ragheef (a flat loaf of bread) until he passed away.'* [121]

On the authority of Samaak who said that I heard al-Nu'maan ibn Basheer say: *'Do you not eat and drink as much as you wish? Whereas I have seen that your Prophet (ﷺ) could not even find a sufficient amount of an inferior quality of date to fill his stomach.'* [122]

On the authority of 'Aa'ishah *(radiyallaahu 'anhaa)* who said, *'The bed of the Messenger of Allaah (ﷺ) was made of animal skin filled with fibres.'* [123]

On the authority of Aboo Burdah, who said: *''Aa'ishah (radiyallaahu 'anhaa) brought out to us a coarse upper garment and lower garment (izaar), and she said that the Messenger of Allaah (ﷺ) passed away in these two.'* [124]

---

120 Reported by al-Bukhaaree and Muslim.
121 Reported by al-Bukhaaree and others.
122 Reported by Muslim.
123 Reported by al-Bukhaaree and Muslim.
124 Reported by al-Bukhaaree and Muslim.

And there are many *ahaadeeth* regarding this.[125]

'Abdullaah ibn 'Umar (*radiyallaahu 'anhumaa*) reported that: '*The Messenger of Allaah (ﷺ) took hold of my shoulder, and said: "Be in this world as if you were a stranger or a passer by." And Ibn 'Umar used to say: "If you live until the evening then do not expect to live until the following morning. And if you live until the morning, then do not expect to see the evening. Take from your health for your sickness and from your life for your death."*'[126]

So hasten, O brother and sister, towards living like the stranger or the wayfarer in your conduct, manners, behaviour, food, drink, housing and in anything else you are able to do so. We should observe and await the arrival to our original abode (Paradise). Therefore we should not expect to live until the morning if we are alive in the evening, and likewise we should not expect to live until the evening if we are alive in the morning. Thus we should not put off repentance, returning back to Allaah and carrying out the rights which are upon us, or even performing a good deed.

We should be conducting ourselves (in our daily lives) as if we can see the scenes of the Day of Resurrection with our own eyes. We should take from our health for our illness and assign our health towards accomplishing acts of obedience as well as to make the most of our lives so that we can be saved from the terrors that follow death.

---

[125] For more on this refer to *Saheeh al-Bukhaaree*, "The book of food", under the section of, what the Messenger of Allaah (ﷺ) and his Companions used to eat; "The book of softening the heart," under the section: How the Prophet (ﷺ) and his Companions used to live. Also refer to *Saheeh Muslim*, "The book of renunciation and heart softening." And also to *Riyaad us-Saaliheen*, chapter 56.

[126] Reported by al-Bukhaaree.

Does the stranger who is away from his country, family, children, kinsfolk and relatives strive in order to build a castle in a foreign land?! Or does the wayfarer live in an isolated cul-de-sac?!

And you - May Allaah have mercy upon you - are a stranger in this world, far away from the home of Paradise, far away from your spouse and children there. And this is only if you are from the people of Paradise. Then how is it if you are from those who do actions of the people of Hellfire and you have no home in Paradise, nor a family nor children, but you have the punishment; an unseen evil waiting for you?!

So beware of leading a life of ease and comfort as Allaah's Messenger (ﷺ) said: *"Beware of leading a life of ease and comfort for verily the (real) slaves of Allaah are not those who live in ease and comfort."*[127]

So necessary for you is *al-Badhaadhah*, as the Prophet (ﷺ) has said: *"Al-Badhaadhah is from eemaan (faith)."*[128] And *al-Badhaadhah* means leading an ascetic and simple life.

## • Having Mercy on the Orphan, Helping him, Stroking his Head and Feeding him

On the authority of Aboo Dardaa (*radiyallaahu 'anhu*) who said: *'A man came to the Messenger of Allaah (ﷺ) complaining of the hardness of his heart. He (ﷺ) said, "Would you like to soften your heart? And to acheive your desire? Then have mercy upon the orphans,*

---

[127] Reported by Ahmad and Aboo Nu'aym in *al-Hilyah*. Our Shaykh said in *al-Mishkaat:* 'Its chain of narrators is good.'

[128] Reported by Ibn Maajah. It is a *saheeh hadeeth* authenticated in *as-Saheehah*.

*stroke their heads, and feed them from your food. Thereby you will soften your heart and acheive your desire.'''* [129]

## • Reducing Laughter

On the authority of Aboo Hurayrah (*radiyallaahu 'anhu*) who related that Allaah's Messenger (ﷺ) said, *"Do not laugh too much, for verily excessive laughter kills the heart."* [130]

## • Fearing that One's Actions will not be Accepted

'Aa'ishah (*radiyallaahu 'anhaa*) said: *'I asked the Messenger of Allaah about the following Aayah:*

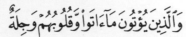

**And those who give (their charity) that which they give with their hearts full of fear.** [131]

*(I asked): "Are these people who commit illegal sexual intercourse, steal and drink alcohol?" The Messenger of Allaah (ﷺ) replied "No, O daughter of Aboo Bakr (or O daughter of as-Siddeeq), they are those who fast, give charity and pray while fearing that their deeds may not be accepted." '* [132]

---

[129] Reported by at-Tabaraanee in *al-Kabeer*. Our Shaykh declared it authentic due to supporting narrations, see *as-Saheehah*.

[130] Reported by Ibn Maajah and others. It is a *saheeh hadeeth*, which our Shaykh reported in *as-Saheehah*.

[131] Soorah al-Mu'minoon (23):60.

[132] Reported by at-Tirmidhee, Ibn Maajah and others. It is a *hasan hadeeth*, which our Shaykh reported in *as-Saheehah*.

# Some Attitudes and Sayings Transmitted about Weeping out of Fear of Allaah and About the Grief and Reminders of the Hereafter[133]

On the authority of Ja'far ibn Burqaan who said: *'I came to know that Salmaan al-Faarisee (radiyallaahu 'anhu) used to say; "Three things make me laugh and three things make me cry. I laugh at the one who is hopeful of the world yet death seeks him; the one who is neglectful (of his Lord) while he is not neglected (by Him); the one who laughs fat the top of his voice, while he does not know whether he is pleasing his Lord or displeasing Him. Three things make me cry: parting from our beloved Muhammad (ﷺ) and his Companions; the terror of the onset of the pangs of death; and the standing in front of the Lord of the worlds while not knowing whether I will be turned towards the Fire or Paradise."'*

Sufyaan ath-Thawree reported that Aboo Dharr al-Ghaffaaree was with al-Ka'b when he said: *"O people, I am Jundub al-Ghaffaaree, hurry to the compassionate brother who gives sincere advice."* The people gathered around him, and he said: *"Do you not know that if one of you intends to go on a journey, then does he not take provisions which will make the journey easier and comfortable for him and enable him to reach his destination?"* They replied *"Of course."* He then said, *"The journey to the Day of Resurrection is longer than (any journey) you intent (to embark upon), so take that which will make your journey easier and comfortable for you."* They asked, *"What is it that will make it easier and comfortable for us?"* He replied, *"Perform Hajj for the terrible things (to come); fast on an extremely hot day, for the duration of the resurrection; pray two rak'ahs in the darkness of the night for the loneliness and coldness*

---

[133] All these sayings are from the book *Hilyatul Awiliyaa'*. I benefited from the book *Rawd az-Zaahideen*, which is a summary of it.

61

*of the grave; say a good word or restrain from bad talk for the standing on the Great Day; and give charity with your wealth in hope that you will be saved from other such (calamities and trials)."*

*"Make in the world two gatherings, a gathering in search for the Hereafter and a gathering in search for the halaal. The third type of gathering will harm you and not benefit you, so do not desire it."*

*"Make your wealth into two dirhams, a dirham you spend on your families in every way you can, and a dirham that you put forward for the Hereafter. The third type of dirham will harm you and not benefit you, so do not desire it."*

*It is reported on the authority of Salaan ibn Abee Mutee' who said: 'A container of water was brought to al-Hasan to break his fast with, but when he brought it close to his mouth he began to weep and said "I remembered the wish of the inhabitants of the Fire in their saying:*

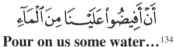

**Pour on us some water...**[134]

*And then I remembered the reply to them.*

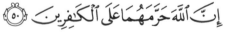

**Surely Allaah has forbidden both (water and provision) to the disbelievers."**[135]

Al-Hasan said: *'Verily you have insufficient time, your actions are sealed, death is looking over you and the Fire is in front of you. And by Allaah whatever you see (i.e. the world) is going. So expect the*

---

[134] Soorah al-A'raaf (7):50.

[135] Soorah al-A'raaf (7):50.

*decision of Allaah every day and night, and let one look to what he has put forward for himself.'*

He also said: *'O son of Aadam! You are nothing but days, whenever a day goes past, a part of you (also) goes.'*

He also said: *'It is befitting for the one who knows that death is his place of arrival, the hour is his appointed time, and the standing in front of Allaah, the Most High, is his place of meeting, that his sadness lengthens.'*

Thaabit al-Banaanee said: *'We were following a funeral procession and we saw nothing but people covering their faces while weeping or covering their faces while reflecting.'*

Al-A'mash said: We were witnessing a funeral, but we did not know who to offer our condolences to because of the grief of the people (i.e., it was so severe and widespread that they did not know where the close relatives of the deceased).

Sufyaan ibn 'Uyaynah said that Ibraaheem at-Taymee said: *'I imagined myself in the Hellfire with its iron chains and blazing fire eating from zaqqoom,[136] and drinking from its zamhareer (a bitterly cold drink), so I said "O my soul, what do you long for?" It replied: "To return to the world and perform a righteous action by which I will be saved from this punishment." I also imagined myself in Paradise with its Hooris[137] dressed in silken garments (of Paradise) with gold embroidery. I said: "O my soul! What do you long for?" It said: "To return to the world and perform a righteous action by*

---

[136] **Translator's note:** A tree in Hellfire with exceedingly bitter fruit.

[137] **Translator's note**: The females of Paradise with wide beautiful eyes who have not been touched by any man or *jinn.*

*which this reward will increase." So I said to myself: "You are in the world and (surrounded by) aspirations."'*

On the authority of Bukayr or Aboo Bukayr that Ibraaheem at-Taymee said: *'The one who is not afflicted with sadness and grief should fear being from among the people of the Fire because the people of Paradise will say,*

**All praises and thanks be to Allaah, who has removed from us grief.'**[138]

It is necessary for the one who does not fear (the punishment of Allaah) to be fearful of not being from among the people of Paradise, because they will say,

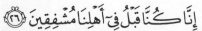

**Aforetime we were afraid with our families (from the punishment of Allaah).**[139]

Zakariyyah al-'Abdee reported about Ibraaheem an-Nakha'ee, that he wept during his illness, and the people said to him: *"O Aboo 'Imraan! What makes you weep?"* He replied: *"How can I not weep while I am waiting for a messenger from my Lord, to inform me whether it is this or that (i.e. Paradise of Hellfire)."*

Hishaam ibn Hassaan said: *'When it was said to Muhammad ibn Waasi', "In what state do you wake up O Aboo 'Abdullaah?" He replied, "What is one to think of a man who moves a stage closer to the Hereafter everyday."'*

---

[138] Soorah al-Faatir (35):34.
[139] Soorah at-Toor (52):26.

# The Fruits of Weeping out of Fear of Allaah

There are abundant fruits from which those who weep out of the fear of Allaah, can reap many benefits. From among them are:

1. Allaah will shade them under his shade on the Day when there is no shade except His.

2. They will not enter the Fire nor will it touch them.

3. They succeed in achieving the love of Allaah, the Most High, as the Prophet (ﷺ) said, *"There isn't a thing more beloved to Allaah, the Most High, than two drops and two marks... a teardrop shed out of the fear of Allaah."*

4. The glad tidings of *Toobah* and the success of attaining Paradise with all its comfort, ease and happiness in the Hereafter.

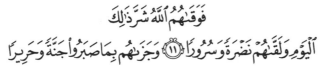

**So Allaah saved them from the evil of that Day and gave them a light of beauty and joy and their recompense shall be Paradise and silken garments, because they were patient.**[140]

5. Uprightness in the world and the taste of the sweetness of *eemaan*.

6. Increase in *eemaan* and guidance.

7. Tranquillity and the peace of the soul.

8. Allaah, the Most High, will make a way out for them and provide them with a good provision from where they could never imagine.

---

[140] Soorah al-Insaan (76):11-12.

**Whoever has *taqwa* (fears Allaah and keeps his duty), He will make a way for him to get out (from every difficulty). He will provide him from sources he could never imagine...**[141]

9.   Allaah, the Most High, will make their affairs easy for them:

وَمَن يَتَّقِ ٱللَّهَ يَجْعَل لَّهُۥ مِنْ أَمْرِهِۦ يُسْرًا ﴿٤﴾

**Whosoever has *taqwa* (fears Allaah and keeps his duty to Him), He will make his affair easy for him.**[142]

10.   They succeed in emulating the Prophet (ﷺ) because weeping out of fear of Allaah is from his (ﷺ) guidance.

11.   They succeed in imitating the Companions (*radiyallaahu 'anhum*) and the pious predecessors because weeping out of fear of Allaah is also from their guidance.

12.   In Paradise, they will take pleasure in remembering their fear and weeping in the world as stated by the Most High:

وَأَقْبَلَ بَعْضُهُمْ عَلَىٰ بَعْضٍ يَتَسَآءَلُونَ

﴿٢٥﴾ قَالُوٓا۟ إِنَّا كُنَّا قَبْلُ فِىٓ أَهْلِنَا مُشْفِقِينَ ﴿٢٦﴾ فَمَنَّ ٱللَّهُ

عَلَيْنَا وَوَقَىٰنَا عَذَابَ ٱلسَّمُومِ ﴿٢٧﴾ إِنَّا كُنَّا مِن قَبْلُ

نَدْعُوهُ إِنَّهُۥ هُوَ ٱلْبَرُّ ٱلرَّحِيمُ ﴿٢٨﴾

**And some of them draw near to others, questioning. Saying: "Aforetime we were afraid with our families (from the punishment of Allaah) but Allaah has been gracious to us, and has saved us from the torment of the Fire. Verily we used to invoke Him before, He is *al-Barr* (the most Subtle, kind, courteous and generous), the most Merciful.**[143]

---

[141]   Soorah at-Talaaq (65):2-3.

[142]   Soorah at-Talaaq (65):4.

[143]   Soorah at-Toor (52):26-28.